The Adventures of Scuba Jack
Copyright 2022 by Beth Costanzo
All rights reserved

What Would You Do?

Making a good choice and doing the right thing, or even knowing right from wrong can be hard! In "What Would You Do" you can practice making hard decisions and have some fun while we explore some everyday dilemmas! Our booklet gives advice on what should be done during confusing or unexpected situations at home, school, or out on your own.

What Would You Do?

You're with friends when they start teasing an unpopular kid, taking his things and calling him names. If you stick up for him, the group could turn on you. You start to walk away, but someone throws you the boy's backpack. What will you do?

What Would You Do?

What Would You Do?

There's a new kid at school who hardly speaks. The other kids are not friendly to him, and they expect you to act the same way. You know this new kid needs a friend. What do you do?

What Would You Do?

What Would You Do?

You're playing with two good friends. They both want to be your best friend. You think you like one friend better. The friend says, "Let's go play by ourselves." You know your other friends' feelings will be hurt if she is left out. What will you do?

What Would You Do?

What Would You Do?

You didn't have time to study for the big test today. There is a girl who sits beside you and always gets 100 percent on her tests. You need a good grade to help bring up your average. Do you copy the girls test or do you talk to the teacher and try to re-take the test another day?

What Would You Do?

_____

_____

_____

_____

_____

_____

_____

_____

What Would You Do?

A person in your class is telling lies about your friend. Do you tell your friend or do you tell a teacher?

What Would You Do?

What Would You Do?

You heard that your two best friends are lying to the principal about who started a fight. Now an innocent person has been blamed. What will you do?

What Would You Do?

What Would You Do?

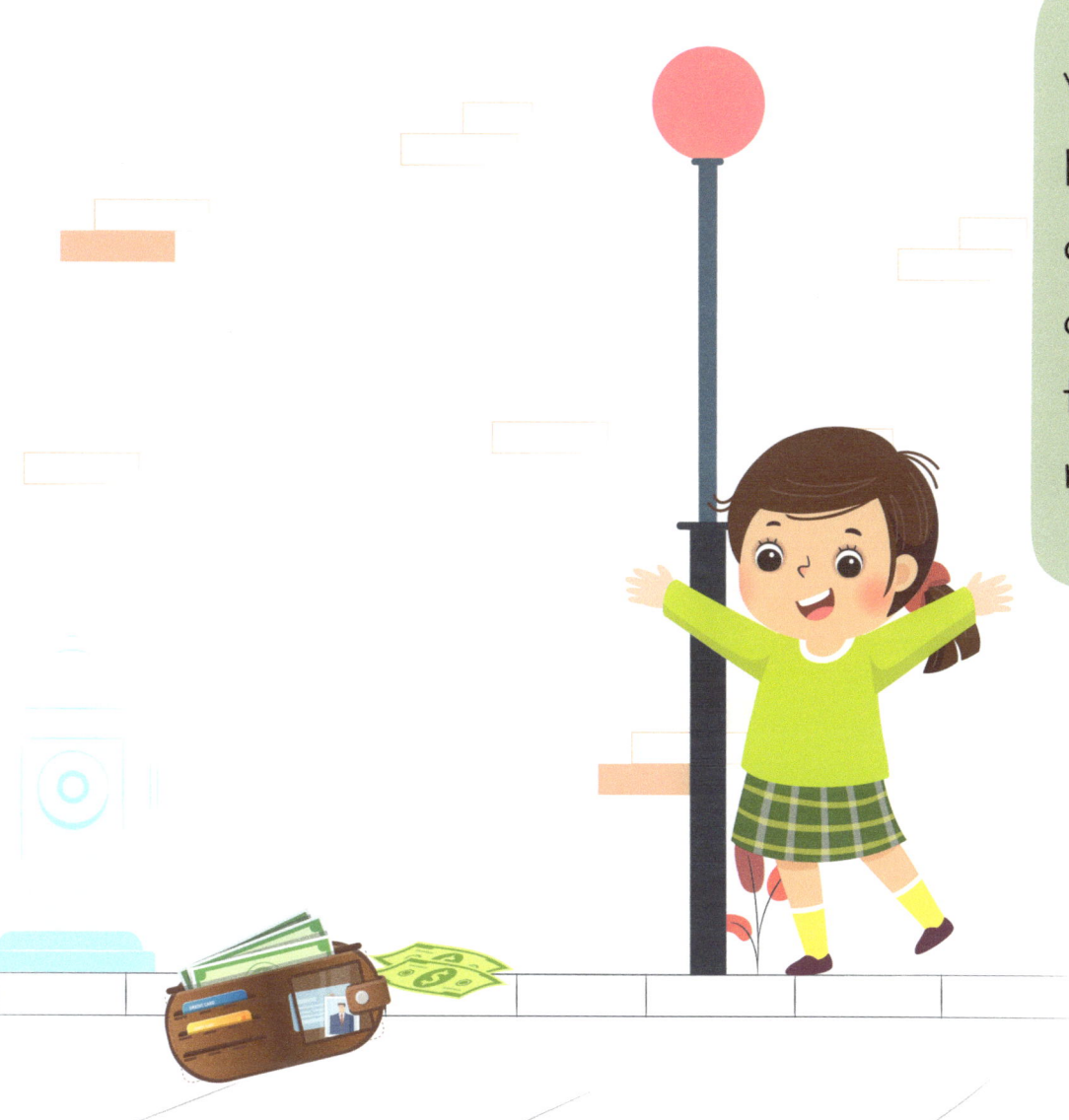

You find a wallet on the street with a lot of money in it. The person who owns the wallet has his name, address and phone number inside. Do you call this person or do you keep the money?

What Would You Do?

What Would You Do?

You see your elderly neighbor drop her groceries on the ground. Your friend laughs and thinks its funny. Do you laugh too, or do you help your neighbor?

What Would You Do?

What Would You Do?

Someone at school forgot their lunch and is hungry. You are not fond of this student, but they asked you to share with them. What do you do?

What Would You Do?

What Would You Do?

You are in a convenience store with a friend that has no money. While you are paying for your soda, you look over and see your friend steal a candy bar.

What Would You Do?

What Would You Do?

You open up a birthday gift from a relative and it is something that you really didn't want.

What Would You Do?

ANSWER KEY

1 - The right thing to do is to give the backpack back. It will not be a popular decision, but it is the right decision. Stand up for the child and make him feel safe.

2 - It is hard to make friends at a new school. Introduce yourself and make him feel comfortable. A friendly, "Hi" can go a long way!

3 - If you came to play with two friends, then you need to play with two friends. One may be more similar to you and easier to get along with, but it's important to make both friends feel included. Keep in mind that it is never fun to feel excluded.

4 - If you didn't study for a test, you should discuss this with your teacher. Explain to him/her that you are not as prepared as you should be and ask if you can take it another day. Cheating on a test is never a good idea.

5 - A person in your class is telling lies about your friend. I would not tell your friend. Instead, I would tell the person spreading lies to stop! Explain to them that If they don't stop, you will tell your parents or a teacher.

6 - Your two best friends are lying to the principal. You should go and talk with the principal. You can ask the Prinicpal to NOT use your name and tell him/her who actually started the fight. No one likes to be blamed for something they did not do!

ANSWER KEY

7 - You should return the wallet to the owner. If the wallet does not have any information inside, then you should return it to the local police station.

8 - You certainly should not laugh when your elderly neighbor drops groceries, but you should help him/her to pick them up. Also, offer to walk the bag of groceries up to the front door. A small act of kindness goes a long way in helping a person

9 - You could give them one of your snacks. Or a small portion of your lunch. Helping others always makes you feel better.

10- You should talk to your friend and tell them that stealing is not "cool." Also, you can get into a lot of trouble and your parents and perhaps the police could be called.

11- You should always be grateful when someone takes the time to buy you a gift. You know what they say, "It's the thought that counts!" Don't forget to say, "Thank You" for their kindness.

www.ingramcontent.com/pod-product-compliance
Lightning Source LLC
Chambersburg PA
CBHW050855010526

44118CB00004BA/173